MAORI CUSTOMS AND CRAFTS

Compiled by ALAN ARMSTRONG

Author of "Games and Dances Of The Maori People",
"Say It In Maori" and "Kiwi Cookbook".

**Viking Sevenseas Ltd; P.O. Box 152, Paraparaumu,
New Zealand**

Haere Mai
'Greetings—Come to me'

Ka patupatu ake taku manawa
'My poor heart is beating faster'

Ka karanga ki te Matua
'Let us call to God above'

The author and publishers wish to thank Mr. Colin Deed for the use of his photographs to illustrate Darts, Games, Garments, Ko, Leaf Boat and Running

SBN 85467 009 2

VIKING SEVENSEAS LIMITED
P.O. Box 152, Paraparaumu, New Zealand
Eighth Printing 1993

ACTION SONG
(*waiata kori*)

The action song is probably the most widely practised and enjoyed of all forms of Maori culture. Not only is it a type of entertainment which is pleasing to eye and ear but it is also an art form which opens a window on Maori music, tradition and language and even on Maori attitudes and aspirations. The action song is essentially a modern development although its origins go back to the *haka waiata* or chanted posture dance of pre-European times. It is therefore a successful adaptation of an ancient art form to present day styles and in its harmonious blending of the old and the new it represents in many ways a summing up of the whole transition of Maori culture from the stone age to the Twentieth Century.

In many action songs the music is an adaptation of a popular European tune but, increasingly, original tunes are being written which, although in the modern idiom, have been written specifically for the Maori words of the song. Even when a 'pop' tune is used however the Maori words are never a translation from English. Words of action songs express the thoughts of the performing group — greeting, farewell, friendship, aspirations for the future and so on. The actions portray, in stylised form, the meaning of the Maori words of the song. We illustrate here some typical actions and their meanings. Women's actions are languid and flowing and without exaggeration or vehemence unless the words themselves require extra emphasis. Men's actions are more vigorous. When performing it is common for the women to stand in front and the men in rear in long rows.

For the person wishing to learn Maori action songs there are books of instruction available but of course there is no substitute for joining a Maori cultural group and learning at first hand. A non-Maori, once he forgets his inhibitions, can acquire expertise as readily as can a Maori.

ADZE
(*toki*)

The adze was a woodworking tool, normally made of hard stone fastened to a wooden handle by fibre. Some highly prized adzes were made from greenstone. The tool was used for such tasks as hollowing out logs for canoe building, and smoothing out timber into planks for building.

AOTEAROA

Aotearoa was the Maori name for New Zealand. Literally it means "long white cloud" (*ao* cloud, *tea* white, *roa* long) although there is dispute about the exact translation as *ao* has a number of meanings. Legends tells of the discovery of New Zealand by the great navigator Kupe in the Tenth Century. Kupe's wife is said to have been the first to sight the land, lying like a white cloud on the far horizon and she called "*He ao! He ao tea!*" The chant was taken up by the others in the canoe who, as they neared the land and saw its full extent, likened it to a long white cloud.

BASKET
(*kete*)

The ancient Maori knew of two types of basket — the strictly utilitarian variety and the esoteric "baskets of knowledge" (*te kete o te wananga*) which were three baskets acquired and brought back to earth by the god Tane after he had visited Io, the supreme being and creator of all things. These three baskets were said to contain all the knowledge of mankind.

The more prosaic Maori basket of everyday usage was seldom ornamented. They were usually woven from one of two common fibres, one formed from flax and the other from the leaves of the cabbage tree, the latter being longer lasting. Other materials which were used were kelp and the barks of various trees. We illustrate a basket made from the bark of the *totara* tree. This is an open basket resembling a modern shopping kit and was known as *patua*. See also kit.

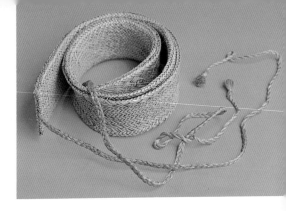

BELT
(*tatua; whitiki*)

The woven belt was an important item of pre-European Maori dress. Indeed in the warmer weather men often wore it as their only garment, to the horror of the early missionaries who considered this most immodest! Often a string was tied to a man's belt and this was used to tie the prepuce over the glans penis (the pre-European Maori male was uncircumcised). Men's belts were plaited from dried flax sometimes alternating light strips with dyed ones to produce a simple design. A more elaborate belt, *tatua pupara*, was doubled over with joined edges which actually formed pockets for small objects rather like a modern money belt! Women's belts were always worn in conjunction with some other garment covering their pubic regions. These belts (*tu*) were also braided from flax, often with the strands in different colours, or from woven strands of sweet smelling *karetu* grass. Early travellers say that women also hung bunches of grass or leaves from the front of their belts.

BIRD SNARE
(*rore; tawhiti*)

Birds were an important source of food and the rain forests of New Zealand provided an abundant supply. They were caught by many methods but the most common was the bird snare which secured the bird whole, often alive and with the feathers (which were used for other purposes) undamaged. Bird snaring was considered an art and the snares were skilfully fashioned. The most common types were the noose snare and the perch snare. The noose snare consisted of a running noose plaited from a strong leaf fibre. These were set up close to streams or drinking troughs and arranged in such a way that the bird had to put its head through the noose to drink and was thereby snared automatically. The perch snare required the bird to alight on a specially constructed perch on which was laid a snare. A hidden watcher would pull on the string and trap the bird around the legs.

BODICE

(*pari*)

In ancient times, Maori women often wore no clothing on the upper part of their bodies in warmer weather or whilst working. There was no shame attached to having the breasts uncovered in those days. In cooler weather they wore a rough cape which hung to the waist and covered the shoulders and back. Sometimes the breasts were exposed, other times the capes were secured with a tie or a curved pin made from bone, wood or shell. In colder weather cloaks were worn fastened across the body.

The gaily decorated bodice which conceals the upper part of the body but leaves the shoulders bare except for supporting straps, is essentially a modern development and is part of the modern Maori dance custom for women. The coloured designs are woven in wool using a tapestry stitch onto tapestry cloth. The woven cloth is then stitched into the bodice proper which is made from red green or black cotton material fastening down the middle of the back. Sometimes the actual design covers only the front of the bodice. Other times it covers around under the arm pits or even reaches to the fastenings at rear. The bodice is supported by plaited shoulder straps and attached to the skirt worn under the *piupiu*.

There are no traditional or tribal designs for these bodices although most designs are based on the *taniko* motif which decorates the woven side panels of many Maori meeting houses. Each cultural group designs its own distinctive motif and groups often incorporate as a frontispiece elements identifying their name such as an initial or a religious symbol such as the crucifix. Other motifs are the crescent moon, stars, *tiki* etc. There are no particular prohibitions on the colours used although black, white and red are the most common.

BURIAL
(*nehu; tapuketia*)
Burial was attended with appropriate ceremony known as the *tangi* (*tangi* to cry). Sometimes the body would be cremated but it was more commonly buried or placed in a cave rock crevice or the branches or hollow trunk of a tree. The remains of important people would be disinterred in later years and the bones placed in a box or hidden. The illustration shows a wooden bone box carved to represent the spirit of the departed ancestor.

CABBAGE TREE
(*ti kouka*)
The cabbage tree or cordyline grows from the low coast to high altitudes. There are various species growing up to eight feet high. To the ancient Maori they were an abundant source of food as both the root and the pith of the trunk are edible. The leaves were much stronger than flax and put to many uses some of which are mentioned elsewhere.

CANOE
(*waka*)
The Maori were a sea faring people. They roamed the waters of Te Moana-nui-a-Kiwa (the Pacific Ocean) and made voyages of thousands of miles through uncharted seas. The great ocean going canoes could accommodate a hundred or more people and their stores and possessions. Such canoes usually had double hulls or had outriggers for stability and frequently a cabin was built on the platform which linked the hulls.

Around the coasts of New Zealand and on its rivers and lakes the Maoris explored, foraged, went to war, fished and disported themselves in craft which ranged in size from large single hull canoes up to eighty feet long down to small hollowed out trunks which only accommodated one or two people. The larger canoes were often elaborately ornamented with high carved prows and decorated sides.

The principal event in the history of the Maori race is the migration by canoe to New Zealand from the legendary homeland of Hawaiiki. Fired by tales of Kupe (see "Aotearoa") and the explorers who followed him there took place a number of waves of migration some of which settled at intermediate points between Hawaiiki and New Zealand and others of which made the full journey over many weeks of danger and privation and guided only by the sun and the stars. These waves of migration culminated in the final migration of the so-called "Great Fleet" which was in no sense a convoy on canoes but a successive series of arrivals spread over the greater part of the fourteenth century. These migrants who were the ancestors of the present day Maori and the inhabitants of the various canoes which settled in different parts of New Zealand were the forerunners of today's tribal groupings.

CARVING

The ancient Maori was an artist and his artistry expressed itself in many forms. Principal amongst these was the art of wood carving or *whakairo rakau*. Wood carving was used to decorate wholly or in part almost all the implements of Maori domestic life from canoes to adze handles. However it reached its highest form in the decoration of buildings, particularly of storehouses and the large meeting houses which were a focal point of Maori social and community life. Carving was used for both the inside and outside of such buildings. Over the course of time and in the various tribal localities, "schools" of carving arose, each distinctive.

In all schools of carving the chief motif was the human figure. Because the head was considered the most important part of the body — the repository of the *mauri ora* or spirit life — it was often carved large in proportion to the remainder of the body. According to traditional belief the ancient carvers believed that only god would create man. Therefore to carve an exact reproduction of the human figure was tantamount to sacrilege. Hence human figures were almost always stylised and to modern eyes appear strangely distorted. In Maori carving curves and loops were common and thus it is often referred to as curvilinear in style in contrast to the rectilinear design of much other Polynesian wood carving. Carving was considered a very sacred operation and attended with appropriate ceremony. Chisels, gouges and adzes were made of rock and greenstone.

CLOAK
(kakahu; kahu)

The cloak was a common form of dress and worn by both sexes. The most popular type reached only to the waist and was convenient for wearing whilst working in cooler weather. The longer cloaks reached to between the knees and ankle and could be wrapped or pinned around the entire body. Sometimes women wore these cloaks pinned just above the breasts leaving the shoulders free. Such cloaks were usually worn at nights or in the colder weather.

The normal material for cloaks was flax but rough cloaks or capes for everyday wear were also made from the tougher fibre of the cabbage tree or from the leaves of the *kiekie*. More elaborate cloaks were made from dogskin or bird skins sewn together. These superior cloaks were ornamented in various ways. Some were covered with bird feathers (see feather cloaks) and others had ornamental borders or were covered with loosely hanging dyed flax thrums. The illustration shows a dog skin cloak.

CLUB
(see kotiate, mere, patu, taiaha)

COMB
(heru)

Maori women generally wore their hair short whilst it was the men who sported long hair. The men followed the Polynesian practice of tying their hair in a large topknot which was often fastened by a quill but sometimes their hair would be tied back or braided. Combs were often worn in the hair for decoration and to keep it tidy. Wooden combs had separate teeth lashed together by flax. The more valuable combs were made from whalebone and some were carved or inlaid with *paua* shells. The elaborately ornamented combs were often family heirlooms.

DANCES

In ancient times dances were an important feature of Maori social and ceremonial life. They were (and are) an expression of emotion — of joy, sadness, welcome or farewell, of tribal or group solidarity and, in less recent times, of divination and preparation for an important event in the life of the village or tribe. Maori dancing was thus largely a team effort being performed by groups and dancing as individuals or in pairs was unknown to the Maori of ancient times.

In contrast to dances of other cultures, those of the Maori were never performed to any accompaniment by either musical instruments or drums. The rhythm was marked only by the stamp of the feet on the ground in perfect unison and by the slap of hands against the body.

The generic term for dances is *haka*. The principal types of dance are the *haka taparahi*, *peruperu*, *powhiri*, *poi* dance, *haka waiata* and the modern action song. The *haka taparahi* was a posture dance usually, but not always, performed by men to a shouted chorus. The *peruperu* was the fierce war dance with weapons; the graceful *haka poi* was performed always by women. In this dance a small ball is twirled in time to the music. The *haka waiata* was a langorous dance to a chanted tune which has been superceded today by the modern action song. Most of these different dances are dealt with in more detail elsewhere in the book, (see also action song, *haka*, music, *poi* dance)

DARTS
(niti teka)

Darts were a toy to the Maori but like many ancient games they had the secondary object of training the warrior-to-be to both throw and to avoid spears hurled in battle. Normally darts were about three feet long and made from stalks of fern or small saplings. There were two techniques for throwing them. One was to throw them with the hand in the same way as for a spear and the other was to propel them by means of the throwing stick to which the dart was attached by a cord with a slip knot.

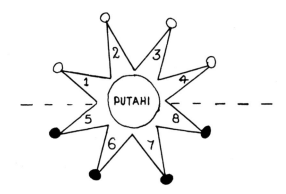

DRAUGHTS

There are many simple games which the Maori used to pass the time of day. One of these is called *mu torere*. Some people claim this is a post European version of the game of draughts since *mu* is said to be a transliteration of the word "move" and is the Maori word for draughts. However there is no reason why a modern word could not have been applied to an ancient game so there is every possibility that *mu torere* is older in its origins than some people suspect. Anyway, to all intents and purposes it is the Maori version of draughts.

The game is played on the star design illustrated on this page. Each player has four stones or counters marked in some way so that he can recognise his own. Player A puts his counters on points 1, 2, 3 and 4. Player B (black counters) places his on the remaining points. The rules are:
(1) Players move alternately.
(2) Players may move a stone into the centre (*putahi*) or on to one of the points of the star BUT only one stone is allowed on each point OR on the centre at the same time.
(3) Players cannot jump over another stone but can only shift a stone to the centre OR to the star point next to it.
(4) For the *first two* moves by either player, only the outer stones, that is the ones on 1, 4, 5 and 8, may be moved as it is NOT permissable to block the other player in the first two moves.
(5) The game is won when one player is blocked by his opponent so that he is unable to move.

EEL
(*tuna*)

The succulent eel has always been a much prized source of food to the Maori. Eels were speared, netted, taken by hand or caught in traps which were woven pots with narrow entrances and inward facing spikes which permitted the eel to swim in but seldom escape. Much time was spent constructing weirs and barriers in various rivers and streams which would direct the eels into the waiting pots. Eels taken by hand were usually caught at night when they could be attracted by the light from blazing torches. Eels were cooked either in a *hangi* or steam oven or wrapped in green leaves and roasted over an open fire. They were always cooked in their skins which were effectively de-slimed by throwing the eel whilst still alive into hot ashes where it would writhe around and rub off the slime into the absorbent abrasive ash.

FAMILY
(*whanau*)

The smallest Maori social unit was the *whanau* or family. However unlike the modern conception of the family, which in the main consists of the parents and the children, the Maori family in the traditional Polynesian manner included all close blood relatives such as grandparents, aunts, uncles, grandchildren etc. A group of familes was a *hapu* or sub-tribe. Groups of *hapu*, all descended from a common ancestor and related by blood ties comprised the *iwi* or tribe. Each *hapu* was led by a chief who in the main ruled by common consent and could be deposed. Over all was the tribal chief of noble birth.

The Maori family unit was close knit. Although women carried out domestic tasks in the main they were accorded due respect by their men and could make their voices heard in the doings of the group. Children were greatly loved by their parents. Young people married in their early twenties, not always having the right of choice. Arranged marriages were common. There was no wedding ceremony in the modern sense although when two persons of high birth were united there was celebration.

FEATHER BOX
(*waka huia*)

Feathers and plumes were used as adornments by the Maori and their uses for decorating cloaks, canoes and the hair have been referred to elsewhere. The black and white tail feathers of the *huia* were particularly prized. Some tribes hold the number twelve in special significance and as the *huia* was said to have twelve tail feathers this added considerably to the importance of feathers from this rare, and now extinct, bird. *Huia* feathers and other small treasures were often held in specially carved containers known as *waka huia* which means literally a repository for the feathers of a *huia*. Some of the larger *waka huia* were in fact used to hold valuable weapons such as a greenstone club and other larger family treasures. As can be seen from the illustration, *waka huia* were often elaborately carved.

FEATHER CLOAK
(*kahu huruhuru*)

Of all the traditional garments of the Maori which have been handed down to this day it is the feather cloak which is the most beautiful and highly prized as a family and personal heirloom. The base of the cloak was made from flax fibre which had been washed, bleached almost white and softened. The women would then roll the fibres together by rubbing them between their thigh and open palm until a long yarn was formed. This was woven into a large rectangle of material which was slightly shaped at the shoulder and at the hips by introducing short rows into the weft at appropriate points. Onto this was fastened the feathers. The most highly prized feathers were those from the *huia* and from the *kiwi*, especially the rare white albino *kiwi*. These feathers were usually used alone to make a complete cloak which was especially valuable. Sometimes the cloak would be fringed with *taniko*, dog's hair or the white *kiwi* feathers. Less prized but more colourful were cloaks made from the feathers of the wood pigeon, which were white from breast and green from the back, from the *kaka* or native parrot, which were red, and from the *tui*, which were a blue-black colour.

FERN

Ferns were used for many purposes. They provided a warm bed, the stalks made darts and were used for decorating and making up the wall panels of the meeting house and, above all, they could be eaten. *Aruhe*, which was the root of the bracken fern, was a staple article of diet which grew anywhere and everywhere and was available all the year round. In themselves the roots were tasteless but by a lengthy process of cooking and pounding they were quite edible especially when combined with other more flavoursome foods. Indeed when rolled into cakes and soaked in *tutu* juice they became quite a delicacy.

The graceful curving scroll of the unfolding fern frond is also present as a design feature in Maori carving, rafter design and personal tattooing.

FISHING
(*huti*)

Kai moana or food from the sea is a favourite with most Maoris today. In pre-European times, without a ready source of meat and a great variety of other food, kai moana, and particularly fish, was one of the staples of the Maori diet. Fish were caught by net and line from the sea and by spears and fish pots, dredges and rakes from fresh water. Fishing was considered as a skill and whilst all members of a tribe might be required on occasion to join in large scale fishing ventures, certain individuals were deemed to have special aptitude in the art and would spend most of their time fishing as well as taking the lead on those occasions when large numbers of the tribe were pressed into service to assist. There were certain prohibitions and rites connected with fishing and during the manufacture of such things as hooks and nets. For example, no food could be eaten during a fishing expedition and certain times were regarded as more propitious for good catches than others. The illustration shows ancient fish hooks. A great deal of patience and skill was required for a manufacture of a good hook from shell, stone, wood or bone.

FLAX
(harakeke; korari)

Phormium Tenax or the native New Zealand flax was probably the most important plant of all to the Maori. Its fibre was put to hundreds of uses. To obtain the fibre, the long broad reddish green leaves were soaked and then scraped and dried. If the fibre needed to be softened it was pounded. It was then plaited into ropes, fishing lines and the like or rubbed together to make yarn which could be woven into clothing and mats. In addition the untreated leaves could be used for plaiting baskets or food containers and plates. See also cloaks; fishing; garments; headband; *piupiu*; rain cape; weaving.

FLUTE

The flute was the most popular Maori instrument and the most capable of producing a variety of musical tones. There are many excellent examples of ancient Maori flutes in museums but little is known of how they are played. An old lady in Porirua, Wellington was thought to be the last exponent of the ancient art of playing the nose flute. Fortunately a commercial recording of her playing was made before she passed away.

There were a number of types of flute, one being the *porutu* which was made from wood with one end closed; *whio* made from wood and played by blowing across the upper end; *koauau* made from wood or bone and played either by the nose or the lips blowing across the open upper end; and finally the *nguru* or whistle flute which was of wood, stone or whale ivory. The *nguru* was short and carved and may have been played by blowing across the open end, although there is some doubt about this. The illustrations show a *putorino*, which is the generic name for flutes played with the mouth, and a *koauau*, which is played with the nose.

FOOD
(kai)

The search for ample supplies of food was one of the principal occupations of the olden time Maori. New Zealand was not a bountiful country compared with the fertile and warm islands of the Pacific which the Maori had left behind. The cultivable food plants which could be brought from their former home were small in number and for the most part the settlers had to depend on what the sea, rivers land and forests of New Zealand could provide. The most important food brought from the ancient homeland was the sweet potato or *kumara* — a food which is still greatly prized by the Maori of today. There is a saying that where the *kumara* flourished so did the Maori. *Taro*, yam and gourd were also brought but did not propagate to the same degree as *kumara*. Foods which were native to New Zealand included the root of the common bracken fern, which provided the starch staple, the flesh and roots of various other plants and trees, various flowers, berries and fungi, birds and their eggs, dogs, bats and the large native rat or *kiore* and all the multitudinous food from both salt and fresh water including fish, shellfish and even seaweed.

All cooking was done by women. Only when compelled by necessity would a man cook for himself. The most common method was cooking by steam in a small pit scooped from the ground but other methods included roasting over an open fire and, where the natural resources permitted it, cooking in hot pools and thermal steam.

GAMES
(mahi rehia)

Many of the Maori games of old were similar to those which children of other races have played throughout the centuries. They included kite flying, top spinning, and sports such as jumping, swimming, boxing and wrestling — to mention but a few. There were also other games which are more peculiarly Maori or Polynesian such as hand games and stick games. Many of these latter types of game, as well as being forms of amusement, were designed to teach and foster the arts of war. See also darts; draughts; hand games; jackstones; jumping jacks; kites; leaf boats; sled etc.

GARMENTS

When they came to New Zealand from the warmth of the central Pacific the Maoris had to adopt a much heavier form of clothing, at least for the colder weather and at nights. Even so, they dressed very scantily by modern standards. The principal textile was woven from the fibre of the ubiquitous and versatile flax plant.

Basically there were two main garments, the kilt which covered the lower part of the body and the cloak which covered the upper part of the body. The kilt for men was sometimes quite abbreviated consisting merely of a triangle of cloth with a string at the apex which passed through the crotch and tied on to the waistband at the rear. From the accounts of early explorers however it would seem that community modesty only required men to keep the glans penis covered from view and thus men would sometimes discard their lower garment entirely and wear only a belt or a string from which hung another string which fastened the prepuce over the glans. Female modesty however demanded the the pubic area always be covered and women habitually wore a kilt which reached anywhere from lower thigh to ankle.

The ordinary cloak was well made and unornamented. Ceremonial cloaks were more elaborate (see cloaks; feather cloak). They varied from being merely a shoulder covering to being a large mantle which reached from shoulder to ankle and wrapped around the body. The cloak was frequently discarded by both sexes when working or in warmer weather.

Nowadays, the Maori wears European clothing but there is a modern dance costume worn for Maori cultural performances. This consists of the kiltlike *piupiu* (which see) for both sexes and an ornamented bodice for women (v.t.). Both sexes may wear a plaited headband and short ornamented cloak and men may also wear a plaited *tapeka* or sash which crosses over one shoulder and tucks into the waist band of the *piupiu*.

GEYSER

(*puwaiwera*)

The Maoris put to good use geysers and other phenomena of the thermal regions of the North Island. Not only did they provide abundant hot water for bathing and warmth but they provided also a natural steam cooker. The rumbling of the thermal steam was said to be a manifestation of Ruaumoko, the earthquake god.

GODS

(*atua*)

Unlike many primitive people, the Maoris had in their religion the concept of a supreme being known as Io who was credited with supreme power over all other gods and having created all things. Although the existence of Io was kept almost entirely to the priesthood, the concept probably made it easier when the white men came for the Maoris to adapt to Christianity with its concept of the one God.

Next in importance came the six so-called departmental gods such as Tane, god of the forest and birds, and Rongo, god of agriculture. After the departmental gods which were the property of all Maori tribes, each tribe had gods to whom they had exclusive rights. Finally came family gods whose followers were confined to the members of a particular family. Gods were invisible spirits created by the power of abstract thought and hence of uncertain form. Thus the gods had to have human mediums or interpreters without which they could not exist. These were the members of the priesthood or *tohunga* (from *tohu* to guide) .These experts in religious theory and ritual were graded accorded to the class of god which they served, (see also legends, mythology).

GODSTICKS
(*tiki wananga*)

Godsticks were wooden sticks about eighteen inches long, sharpened at one end and carved at the other in the form of a head or whole image. They served as temporary dwelling places for gods. They were the most important man-made symbols of supernatural power and figured prominently in Maori religious ritual although they were not worshipped or regarded as a sacred thing in themselves. The godstick would usually be thrust into the ground in front of the priest and would then serve as the material vehicle for the god, which would speak through the human medium. When used in ritual, godsticks were often bound with flax fibre cord, smeared with *kokowai*, the sacred red ochre, and dressed with feathers. Following this, the godstick was ready to be entered by the *atua* or spirit. The godstick is one of the few material tools of Maori religion which existed largely as an abstract philosophy, without the visible paraphernalia of other religions, see also gods.

GOURD
(*hue*)

The gourd plant was one of few items of vegetation which the Maori brought to New Zealand from Hawaiiki. The plant was steamed and eaten, but principally it was grown to provide containers for water and for preserved birds. When used for water a round hole was pierced in the vegetable near the stalk end and the inside was removed leaving the hard rind. As a water container the gourd was called *taha*. As a food container it was *taha huahua*. Large gourds were used for this purpose with the stalk end cut off to make an opening large enough to insert cooked birds. The cooked birds were packed inside in layers and melted bird fat poured in to fill the spaces. Often the gourds would be decorated with patterns.

GREENSTONE
(*pounamu*) (see jade)

HAKA

Haka is the Maori word meaning a dance of any kind. In practice and in modern usage however it has come to mean the two types of vigorous shouted posture dances performed only by men. These two dances are actually the *haka taparahi* and the *peruperu*. *Haka taparahi* is a vigorous dance to a shouted chanted tune. Many people erroneously assume that *haka taparahi* is a war dance but actually the words can express the whole gamut of public and private sentiment such as welcome and farewell, a grievance or complaint or even a prayer to one of the ancient Maori gods. Private sentiments include exultation at the act of love and triumph at escape from capture such as *Ka Mate*. The words of *Ka Mate* are below. The *peruperu* is the true war dance. It is similar in form to *haka taparahi* but is performed with weapons.

Ka mate is one of the best known *haka taparahi*. It was chanted by the famous warrior chief Te Rauparaha after he had been saved from his enemies. The translation is a very free one as a literal rendition would require a number of background notes:

Ka mate! Ka ora!	First 'twas death, but now 'tis life again for me
Tenei te tangata puhuruhuru	Behold the brave man
Nana nei i tiki mai	Who saved me
Whakawhiti te ra!	And caused the sun to shine once more
Aue upane! Aue kaupane!	I ascend to freedom
Whiti te ra	Into the light of day

HAND GAMES
(*mahi ringaringa*)

In days gone by the traditional games of the Maori were not only social amusement to pass the idle hours in harmless fun but they were also designed to inculcate the quickness of hand and eye which were most necessary for the warrior-to-be. Hand games are one of the traditional games which have been passed down and still played by Maori children.

Position 1
Hands on hips

Position 2
Forearms raised,
fists clenched

Positions 3 & 4

One fist raised, the other on hip

Most hand games are played between two people although some can be played by a larger group. The games consist of a rapid series of actions made by the hands and arms, and sometimes the body itself, in time to a chanted call. Naturally there were considerable variations in calling and actions between the versions practised by various tribes, however nowadays the games have become more stereotyped. We illustrate and describe a simplified version of a very popular hand game known as *Hei Tama tu Tama*. If played with speed and vigour and a swaying of the hips it can be quite tiring and challenging even though there are only four basic positions. Experienced players often evolve variations on the positions.

Method of Play

(1) The game is played with two players facing one another. Both players adopt position 1.

(2) One player challenges the other with the call *Hei tama tu tama*! and the other accepts by calling *Ae*! (Yes).

(3) The challenger then goes into his first movement which may be any one of positions 2, 3, or 4. At the same time he calls out *Hei tama tu tama*! Simultaneously the other player also makes an action.

(4) If the second player's action is the same as the one which the challenger makes, then he has won the round and gets the right to begin the next round. If he makes a different action from the challenger he loses the round and the challenger starts the next round.

For all rounds after the first one the player who is the challenger draws out the *Heiiiiiii* to a considerable length. This is the warning to the other player he is about to make his move and then on *tama* both players move.

Scoring

There are two methods of scoring:

(1) The winner is the player who reaches first and wins the tenth round, or

(2) The winner is the player who first wins ten rounds (each player keeps his own score).

HANGI

A *hangi* is the Maori oven in which food is cooked by steam. First firewood is piled over a shallow pit and round rocks placed on top of the wood. As the latter burns away, the heated stones sink slowly into the pit. Finally the burning wood is removed, water is sprinkled on the stones to make steam, food is placed in containers on top of the stones and then the whole is covered with leaves and finally dirt to seal in the steam. The food then cooks for three to four hours.

HEADBAND

(tipare)

The headband illustrated is essentially a modern development and worn by women as part of the modern ceremonial dance costume (see garments). In olden times Maori women generally wore their hair quite short. The modern headband is made in much the same way as the bodice (which see), being stitched in coloured wool onto tapestry cloth. The designs usually follow the *taniko* pattern and are complementary to the bodice design.

To Make a Flax Headband

(1) Take two long flax leaves and divide each in half lengthways. Cut off the inner rib and the outer edges so the four strips are the same width.

(2) To begin, fold the flax as in figure one. To help you it is best to mark the ends with A, B, C and D as shown.

(3) Plait A under C and over D.

(4) Bend B across A and D and under C, see figure 2.

(5) Bend B over C and under D.

(6) Bend C over D and B and under A, see figure 3.

(7) Continue as follows: C over A and under B; A over B and C and under D; A over D and under C; D over C and A and under B.

(8) Repeat as in (7) for the entire length required. If you do not have sufficient length with the pieces you are using, take the other two pieces and plait into the pattern, placing a new strip of flax onto the top of a horizontal strip.

(9) To join the headband at the end, place the beginning of the article under the loose ends and weave them into the pattern.

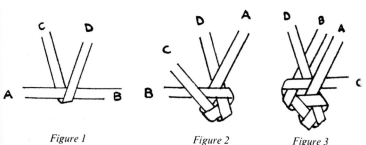

Figure 1   Figure 2   Figure 3

HEITIKI (*see tiki*)

HINEMOA AND TUTANEKAI

HISTORY
(*nga korero o mua*)

The origin of the Maori race is shrouded in mystery. One theory is that their first homeland was in central Asia. From there the Polynesian peoples spread down through the Malay peninsula into the scattered islands of the central Pacific. One of these islands was the traditional homeland which today we know only by the name of "Hawaiiki". From this homeland the ancestors of the Maori set out on their voyages of discovery and migration throughout the Pacific. The islands of New Zealand were probably the last to be discovered. Most traditions honour Kupe as the discoverer. Some time about the tenth century A.D., Kupe and his brother Ngake who was in another canoe, made landfall around North Cape then sailed around the North Island and through Cook Strait, stopping at several places. Kupe returned to Hawaiiki and gave his people an enthusiastic description of the fertile land which he had discovered.

In Hawaiiki there was overcrowding, lack of food and internal quarrels. Fired by tales of Kupe and other explorers who had followed him, the more adventurous families began a migration to New Zealand. There are some accounts which state that when the Polynesians arrived they found in New Zealand a race of inferior people, possibly of a Melanesian type. These were either absorbed or wiped out by the newcomers but this story of an original people cannot be substantiated. The first Maori settlers were the crews of three canoes. The second wave of settlers came in two canoes captained by Toi and Whatonga. They introduced new blood and intermarried with the people already there. From this time on various canoes arrived from Hawaiiki culminating in the great migration of the fourteenth century. This was the most famous event in Maori history because all tribes today trace their ancestry to the crews of these canoes.

The Maori people continued to multiply until the coming of the white man at the end of the eighteenth century. Although there were some areas of conflict, the Maoris in most cases received the early white settlers hospitably and in friendship until the avarice for land of the increasing flood of Europeans brought about the wars of the late nineteenth century. Subdued to a certain extent, but never conquered by the white man, the Maori people began to adapt to European ways and values and to increase in numbers from the state of near decimation brought about by a combination of the wars and the diseases introduced by the white man.

The integration of the two races produced many stresses and strains which left their mark on the emerging racial partnership but now, 150 years later, New Zealanders are by and large two races but one people and Maoris live, work and play in the same manner as all other citizens.

HONGI (see legends)

Hongi is often referred to as "kissing the Maori way". In fact kissing in its modern form was probably unknown to the pre-European Maori and the *hongi* was not really a mark of affection so much as a form of greeting more akin to the modern shaking of hands. It is not a "rubbing of noses" as many people think but a light pressing together of noses first on one side and then on the other. Another sign of friendship and protection similar in intent to the *hongi* is to double the forefinger of the right hand and to place the projecting second joint to the tip of the nose.

HUI

The word *hui* means "to meet" or "to congregate together". Nowadays it refers to any large gathering of Maoris for the purpose of celebration. One of the best known is the *hui topu* which is an annual gathering of Maori Anglicans in the Waiapu diocese for the purpose of cultural competition and spiritual renewal.

IDOLS

Unlike many primitive peoples, the Maori did not worship idols or give their gods any tangible form, (see gods).

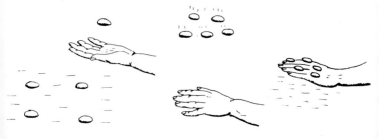

JACKSTONES

Jackstones, or knucklebones, as it is often called today, was also one of
the traditional games of the Maori. It was played with small round stones
or berries. Five was the number which featured in many games but there
are stories of skilled adults playing with up to fifteen objects at a time.
Knucklebones was not only a child's game but was played also competi-
tively by adults either in pairs or in family and village teams.

We give now a South Island tribal version of the game called *koruru*:

(1) Four stones are laid out in a square on the ground. The fifth stone is
thrown with one hand, see figure 1, and then the same hand scoops up two
stones and catches the falling fifth stone. Holding two of the stones still in
the same hand, the fifth stone is thrown yet again and whilst it is airborne
the remaining two stones are scooped up and the fifth stone caught.

(2) The four stones are replaced on the ground and the fifth one is thrown
up. Whilst airborne, the four are scooped up before the descending stone
is caught.

(3) The four stones are placed again in a square and the fifth stone is
thrown up. Each time it is airborne the throwing hand scoops up one of
the four stones and places it to the middle of the square before catching
the fifth stone. Finally the four stones are scooped up together whilst the
fifth is airborne.

(4) Begin with all five stones in the hand. Throw one up, place the other
four out in a square then catch the falling stone.

(5) Throw all five stones and catch on the back of the hand, see figures 2
and 3. This should be continued until all five are caught.

(6) Leave one stone on the ground and retain four in the hand. Throw up
the four, pick up the fifth with the throwing hand, and catch the four in
the same hand as they descend. The winner is the individual or the team
which first completes all movements correctly.

JADE
(*pounamu*)

New Zealand jade varies in colour from white to near-black but it is most often found in various shades of green, hence its popular name "greenstone". It comes from certain boulders found mainly in rivers in the South Island. In addition however to its comparative rarity it was valued for its hardness and beauty when polished. It was used only to make the most prized and valued objects and to fashion it into weapons, tools and ornaments took many hours of painstaking work.

JUMPING JACK
(*karetao; karari*)

The jumping jack was a Maori toy which resembles the European puppet. Jumping jacks varied in size, the normal being fifteen to eighteen inches long, but there are accounts of some made to actual man size. They were carved from wood in human form with a hand grip at the base. The arms were carved separately and attached to the body by means of cord passed through holes in the shoulders of the figure. The cord ends were fastened at the back of the toy and the owner, by manipulating the string, would cause the arms to move in various directions. By shaking the figure at the same time a fair imitation is obtained of someone performing the *haka taparahi* (which see) or posture dance.

Some of the jumping jacks currently preserved in museums are well finished, with quite elaborate carving and decoration, particularly those representing the tattoo of the man's face. Unlike most other Maori carving some of the jacks were a very close reproduction of the human form even down to well carved genitals. When the jumping jacks were made to "dance" the owner sang songs which were peculiar to this activity.

KAURI

The *kauri* tree was native to New Zealand's North Island. It belongs to the pine family and was especially favoured by the Maori for carving, building and canoe making because of its hard durable trunk. The grey smooth bark could also be peeled from the tree in large sheets and was used by the Maori for various purposes.

KILT

Both sexes covered the lower part of their body with a kilt like garment. The most common was a short skirt known as *rapaki*. Another type, normally worn by men going to war was called *maro*. It was triangular and either worn singly with a string passing from the apex through the crotch and fastening at rear to the waistband, or two were worn at front and rear and joined at the apices. The woman in our picture is wearing a type of kilt known as *maro kopua* which was usually worn only by young women of superior family. *Maro* and *rapaki* were generally made of dressed and woven flax.

KITE

(*manu tukutuku; pakau; kahu*)

Kite flying was by no means confined to children. Indeed the best kites, made with loving care and much expenditure of labour and materials, were owned and flown by adult men and occasionally there would be kite flying contests. Children generally played with small, easily constructed kites made from common materials. Most Maori kites were fashioned in the shape of a large bird with outstretched wings. A framework was made from light split saplings or reeds and the common ones were covered with the leaves of the *raupo*. The strings of these common kites were made from split flax leaves tied together. The superior kites owned by adults however were much more elaborate. The frames were often covered with bark and sometimes the head was carved in simple fashion. The kite would sometimes be decorated with dog hair and brightly coloured feathers. In some cases strings of shell were attached to a kite to make a rattling sound.

Kite flying Maori fashion was accompanied by special recited charms. Some of these were to encourage the kite to gain height and to fly well. Others were chanted as the kite descended so that it would land gently and without damage. As the bigger kites measured as much as fifteen feet across they had be launched by helpers from a hill side whilst the owner manipulated the strings from below. To bring a kite to earth it was considered unlucky to haul in the string because this caused the kite to swoop down. The usual method was for a helper to walk along under the cord pressing it down with his hand until the kite was gradually lowered to earth.

Illustrated is a typical Maori pre-European kite which any competant do-it-yourselfer could reconstruct and try out. The body is made from flax leaves cut in half down their length and trimmed to size. These are fastened together with cord, string or fibre (if you want to be completely authentic). Balance and aerodynamic properties are given by adding feathers to the nose and tail and large sprigs of brushwood or, better still, the plumes of the *toetoe* or "Prince of Wales" feathers. The string for holding the kite should be attached to the centre of the body.

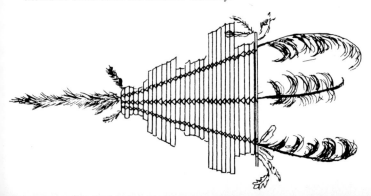

KIT
(*kete*)

Nowadays when people think about Maori kits they do not have in mind the ancient baskets but the modern plaited kits usually made from flax and suspended from two looped handles. These are a common shopping accessory made and used by Maori women. Frequently, dyed flax in bright colours is also woven into the kit to form attractive geometric designs. The more elaborate the design, the more prized is the kit.

When making a kit the flax should always be freshly cut for the task as the dried article is too stiff to weave satisfactorily and may break at points where it has to be bent or twisted. The flax blades must be stripped into even widths and the fleshy lower ends removed.

The kits or baskets of ancient times were usually without ornamentation and strictly utilitarian but occasionally a kit was made to hold some treasured object, or to be carried by the high born, with ornamentation usually in the form of feather or dog's fur decoration. Sometimes a superior plaited article would be made using dyed flax woven into the kit to form a *taniko* design.

KIWI

This flightless bird which is almost sightless and comes out only at night has curiously become a symbol of the New Zealander. Today it is protected and very rare. The pre-European Maori hunted it with dogs and prized it as a delicacy and for its curious dun-coloured spiny feathers which were used for ornamenting superior cloaks.

KO

The *ko* was the most important of Maori agricultural tools. The longer *ko*, which were sometimes even carved, were about ten feet long and used for breaking up the soil. The shorter article was about six foot long and used in cultivating work. The blade in both models was narrow. The *ko* was also used in digging holes for posts and excavating soil for the elaborate earthworks which surrounded Maori defended villages. The *taka* or footrest gave additional push to penetrate the soil.

In breaking in new ground or digging up fern root a number of men would often work together standing behind one another in a row so that a long section of earth was broken. In preparing the soil for planting however, a different technique was used. Only the soil where the plant was to go was broken. The *ko* was used as a lever and thrust into the ground and levered up to displace the soil. This was done three times so that a triangular clod was thrust up. This was pounded with a wooden club and roots and stones removed. Finally the finely worked soil was piled into small mounds ready for the seed or tubers as the case might be. Planting the sweet potato was regarded as a very sacred rite and was attended with ritual and ceremony and many incantations.

KOTIATE

The *kotiate* was a type of Maori club with a wide flat blade and a notch in either side of the blade. The usual material was whalebone or hard rock. The elaborately carved wooden weapon was probably a post-European development, primarily intended for gift or sale. The traditional *kotiate* was only carved at the end of the handle in a spiral design meant to resemble the human head; see also *patu*.

KOTUKU

The *kotuku* was the rare white heron which was found mostly in the swamps of the South Island. So elusive was the bird that the Maoris used the phrase *He kotuku rerenga tahi* (the white heron of a single flight) to describe a visitor who came rarely.

KOWHAI

This beautiful native tree with its fern-like foliage and golden yellow pea-like flowers grows to thirty feet and is a native of New Zealand. Some varieties have lemon-green or lime-green flowers and others have an orange flower. The sweet nectar from the flower attracted the birds which the Maoris loved to trap and families and villages would know the exact location of the *kowhai* trees in the forests which surrounded their home area and would lay their bird snares accordingly.

LANGUAGE
(korero Maori)

The Maori language is still widely used amongst Maoris in their homes and on Maori ceremonial and social occasions. It is a subject at University level and is taken in public examinations by a large number of pupils each year in certain schools. It is in reality a dialect of the language spoken throughout Polynesia and therefore has an recognisable affinity with most languages spoken in the Pacific and even similarities to such Asian languages as Malay and Indonesian. For example if we take the Maori word for "stone" *whatu*, we find that it is *vatu* in Fijian, *fatu* in Samoan, *batu* in Malay and *patu* in the Caroline Islands dialect. Such similarities extend to many words and to general grammatical construction. Within the Maori language itself there are also differences between tribes and districts but these do not constitute separate dialects or prevent Maoris throughout New Zealand understanding one another and such differences are lessening as the years go by and the language is taught in schools.

The Maori language is phonetic in that it is pronounced to all intents and purposes as it is spelled. There are fifteen letters which includes *ng* and *wh* because these form single sounds not exactly represented in English. Other consonants are h, k, m, n, p, r, t, w and the vowels are a, e, i, o, u.

The vowel sounds are much more pure (there are no dipthongs) and rounded than the English equivalent. Each has a long and a short sound, *approximately* as follows:

a — long as in *mark* or short as in c*u*t
e — long as in *ai*r or short as in b*e*t
i — long as in f*ee*d or short as in f*i*t
o — long as in f*o*rk or short as in v*io*let
u — long as in sp*oo*n or short as in s*oo*t

In written Maori the long sound is denoted by doubling the vowel or placing a macron above the single vowel e.g. kākā.

Consonents are pronounced as in English except that there is no rolling of "r"; "t" is more forward on the tip of the tongue; "wh" is an aspirated w (hw as in *wh*en)in some tribal areas and pronounced as a straight "f" sound in others; "ng" is a nasalised sound as in si*ng*ing and must not be pronounced as a straight "n" or as the "ng" in "fi*ng*er.

LEAF BOAT
(*waka rau*)
Many simple games were enjoyed by Maori children. Toys were usually quickly made and little time was spent on elaborate construction. A popular toy was the small fragile leaf canoe made from leaves of the flax and provided with a stick for a mast onto which was fastened another leaf which acted as the sail. Racing with leaf canoes was a popular pastime.

LEGENDS
(*korero purakau*)
The imaginative, colourful and often touching legends of the Maori people are an important aspect of their cultural heritage. Many such legends appear to be variants on similar tales from other parts of Polynesia and it is obvious that they were passed down by successive story tellers and gradually changed and embroidered to fit in with local New Zealand scenes, personalities and events. Unlike myths, legends usually have some basis of fact and for people without a written language they were a means of perpetuating history which in other cultures would have been transcribed and passed on with little variation. Because Maori history was essentially verbal before the coming of the missionaries and their transformation of Maori into a written language, there is bound to be variation in such history and an element of unreliability. However from the legends it is possible to piece together some detail of the origins and continuing story of the race down to these modern times.

Other legends and stories were a means of spreading abroad tales of heroism, of war and peace and of the gossip of the tribe and its affairs. Famous chiefs and their doings figure a great deal in such stories and of course, as the Maori people were no exception to the maxim that all the world loves a lover, there were many stories and legends of love and lovers One of the best known and most frequently recounted of such legends was. that of Tutanekai and Hinemoa. Unlike many other such stories it is undoubtedly grounded on a solid basis of fact.

Hinemoa was a chieftainess of the sub tribe which lived on the shores of Lake Rotorua. In this lake was the island of Mokoia on whom was another well born, but unfortunately illegitimate, young man named Tutanekai. The tribes of the two young people sometimes visited one another for social occasions and thus Hinemoa and Tutanekai had come to know and love one another. The affair had had to be pursued very discreetly and had progressed little beyond clandestine hand holding and a mutual declaration of affection. At night however Tutanekai would sit on the verandah of his house which was on a hillside over-looking the lake and would play his flute. A gentle breeze often wafted the sounds of the music to Hinemoa as she stood on the lake shore. It was reputed that skilled flute players could breathe words into their instruments and Hinemoa could sense the declaration of love which the music contained.

However, as often happens on such occasions, the path of true love did not run smoothly. Hinemoa's relatives suspected that she had fallen in love with Tutanekai and whilst they considered him a nice young man he was after all . . . ! That every night they ensured that the canoes were well beached so that Hinemoa would be unable to pull them into the water on her own and go to her lover. One night as Hinemoa stood there and listened to the plaintive melody of Tutanekai's flute she felt she could bear it no longer and casting her clothes aside in order to swim unencumbered she dived into the lake and guided by the music she swam the long journey to Mokoia Island. When she finally reached the island, cold and exhausted, she realised that she was naked and her natural shyness asserted itself. Just beyond the beach she came upon a hot pool and entered it.

Some time later she heard footsteps and the shadowy figure of a man filled a calabash with water from a cold spring next to the pool. Hinemoa imitated a man's voice and called gruffly "Who is the water for?" The water-bearer answered: "I am the slave of Tutanekai. The water is for my master." Whereupon Hinemoa's hand came out of the darkness, seized the calabash and broke it against the rocks. The startled slave raced back to Tutanekai and reported the strange happening. Tutanekai was too tired to worry and send the slave back for more water. Several times more the slave had his calabash taken from him and broken until at last Tutanekai strode down to the pool himself to take action against this impudent intruder. He groped around the edges of the pool until he caught an arm and pulling on it drew Hinemoa out into the moonlight. He stared at her and then took her into his arms and led her back to his house.

The next morning the lovers slept late and when at last Tutanekai's father sent a slave to wake him, the fellow reported back that peeping through the doorway he had seen not two feet but four! Thereupon Hinemoa and Tutanekai emerged and their union was acclaimed by the tribe. The descendants of Hinemoa and Tutanekai live in Rotorua today and the island of Mokoia and its story of love is a favourite spot with tourists.

MANAIA

The *manaia* was the so-called "bird-headed man" of traditional Maori carving design. Basically it was the human image with the head in profile and coming to a point which gives the appearance of a beak. Sometimes the head portion only was used as a separate design to replace the hands and feet of an otherwise normal figure. Some authorities suggest that the design might have originated from an ancient bird cult. It was much used in the carved barge boards of canoes and for the door and window lintels of carved buildings.

MAORI

The Maoris of New Zealand (including the Cook Islands) are, in effect, a tribe of the Polynesian race which is to be found throughout the Pacific. Their racial characteristics are a stocky, strongly built physique which is somewhat shorter proportionately in the lower leg than the European, black hair which is generally wavy but sometimes 'frizzy', a broader nose and slightly fuller lips than the European and an original skin colour which was probably medium to darkish brown. First cousins to the Maori are the people of Hawaii, Tonga, Samoa and the Tahitian Islands. More distantly related are the Melanesian people of Fiji and the Solomon Islands who generally are taller, darker and with 'frizzy' hair and the Micronesian people of the Caroline Islands and Gilbert and Ellice Islands.

When the white and or *pakeha* came to New Zealand, the Maoris had no name for themselves. Early writers referred to them as "natives", "aborigines" and "New Zealanders". Later they used the word *maori* which in their language meant "usual" or "normal" to refer to themselves as a race and as a nation, (see also language; history)

MARAE

The word literally means an expanse of anything. Thus *marae roa* or the long expanse was the ocean. Normally however the word was applied to the large open space or village green where social observances were conducted in a Maori commuity. Nowadays it refers to any place where Maoris gather but specifically to the large open space in front of a carved Maori meeting house. In ancient Maoridom, (and also in this present day) guests were welcomed and farewelled on the *marae*. Here the tribal chiefs and speechmakers addressed the people and all free men had the chance to agree or disagree with the opinions of their leaders. It was the setting of the councils of war and peace, indeed the heart of the community.

MARRIAGE

Amongst common people in ancient Maoridom there was no marriage ceremony as such. A young man and woman would form an attachment and later this would be recognised as a permanent union. The sexual experimentation of single life would then cease and eventually children would be born. Sometimes married couples would find themselves incompatible and would separate but once children were born there was strong social pressure from parents and tribe to hold the union together.

Amongst those of superior birth, marriages often had a political end and particularly amongst chiefly families were arranged affairs by the parents. Here the marriage was more formal and although there was no "wedding" as we know it today there would be an assembly of the families of the two people concerned, a betrothal, an exchange of gifts and finally feasting when time came for the couple to actually live together. Sexual freedom came to an end upon marriage and if either party transgressed the families and sub-tribes would take action and on some occasions war was said to have resulted. The couple normally settled with the husband's people and either lived with them for a time or made their own home close by, (see also virgin)

MEETING HOUSE
(*whare tapere*)
In New Zealand today, one of the most visible manifestations of Maori cultural heritage is the Maori meeting house. These large houses, many of which are carved and elaborately decorated inside and out, dot the country but are more common in the North Island and particularly in the Northern Central and Eastern parts of the island. Some are of long history and others are modern with all modern conveniences. The construction of meeting houses continues to this day and expresses the pride of Maori communities in their past and their confidence in the future. When a Maori builds a meeting house he is giving tangible expression to his pride of race or *Maoritanga*. In former times, as in this modern age, the meeting house and its marae (which see) were a focus for community life and tribal intercourse and cooperation. It served as a hostel for visitors, a house for gossip and amusement at night and in bad weather, and a forum for the important decisions of corporate life.

MERE
The *mere* is one of the three types of short club. The *mere* type was the simplest form being shaped rather like a short paddle, broad and flat at the striking end and narrowing to a circular portion for holding in the hand. The *mere* was made in stone, whalebone and greenstone but to be strictly accurate the term *mere* should only be applied to the greenstone version of the club. Clubs made from other material in the *mere* shape actually have their own names. The greenstone *mere* was always ground much thinly than clubs made from stone because the jade is so tough that it can be ground finely without risk of its breaking or chipping. The term *meremere* is also found. This usually refers to the more modern and often finely carved club made from hardwood in the paddle shape.

MOA

Little is known about this large, almost pre-historic bird. A model of the *moa* in the Dominion museum shows a large ostrich-like bird about ten feet tall. It is a reconstruction from bones which have been unearthed. A notice beside the model states that it is thought that the bird seldom walked upright as shown in the model but with the neck bent over rather as an ostrich walks. It has sturdy feet with sharp talons and probably had ceased to fly long before the Maori came to New Zealand.

The term *moa* was applied to the domestic fowl in the Polynesian islands of the Pacific. This fowl was not introduced to New Zealand and it is obvious that the first settlers used the word therefore to apply to the bird they found on these shores on their arrival and which furnished an even better source of meat than the *moa* they had known in their homelands. It would appear that the *moa* survived in the South Island long after it was extinct in the North but even so it had probably died out in New Zealand before the arrival of the third and main wave of migration and accounts of the bird in Maori tradition are sparse.

MOKO *(see tattoo)*

MUSIC
(waiata)

Waiata actually means "song". The songs of olden times were divided into a number of types, each with their own Maori name, according to the reason for their composition. Thus we have such classifications as lullabies (*oriori*), abusive songs (*patere*), work songs (*tewha*), laments (*waiata tangi*) and so on. To a Maori the use of chant or song to express emotion was commonplace and appropriate and nothing was considered too trivial to serve as the theme of a song. Thus day-to-day happenings as well as historical occasions were commemorated in songs which often endured long after the event which prompted their writing was forgotten.

Traditional Maori music was chanted. It flowed on almost without break. The range of tones was limited and some of the tonal variation is so minute that it is virtually undetectable by the modern ear. It was devoid of harmony and almost without form. Rhyme was unknown and the requirement of rhythm transcended all else. With religious invocations great importance was attached to the correctness and continuous delivery of the words. At least two people were used for longer chants so that one person would be able to continue the rhythm whilst the other paused for breath.

The old time Maori also had a number of instruments which included castanets, flutes played with mouth and nose, trumpets of shell, wood and bone and a war gong. There was no drum. The stamping of feet provided percussion for dances. All the ancient instruments are now museum pieces and have been abandoned in favour of modern instruments such as the guitar and the ukelele.

With the coming of the white man, Maori music underwent a great change. English, and later American, musical idioms and styles were enthusiastically adopted and adapted at the expense of traditional music. Then Maoris took to writing original music in European style. However even where popular music is used the Maori words are almost never a translation of the English. The music also often undergoes subtle change because it is regarded merely as a vehicle and it is the words which are important, as was the case formerly. Thus many people are often unable to recognise quite popular European tunes when sung and adapted by Maoris with Maori words.

Recently there has been a realisation that the old music and styles must not be discarded. Thus not only has there been a revival of interest in the traditional material which has been preserved but there have also been new chants and *waiata* written in the former idiom. These songs are infused with the new music and have a more modern form and they express the hopes and aspirations of this day as well as commemorating a bygone time. Nevertheless such songs owe much to ancient styles and show a welcome return to a form of the ancient culture which also has relevance to the present day, (see chants; haka; action song).

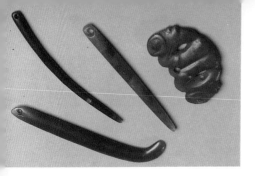

MYTHOLOGY
(*pakiwaitara*)

Before the coming of the European, Maori was not a written language. Thus the stories, folklore and history of the race were passed down by word of mouth. Legend was based on fact, though at times it was hard to see where fact ended and fiction began. Maori mythology was more in the realm of fantasy and concerned the supernatural and spiritual world which was so much a part of the olden time Maori. The mythology of the Maori reveals the depth of thought and religious feeling which is such a vital part of Maori character whilst at the same time being closely allied to nature in all its manifestations. Nowhere are these ingredients better to be found than in the Maori conception of creation, a whole series of myths.

In outline the myths tell of long ages of night until at last Rangi the Sky Father and Papa the Earth Mother emerged from the womb of the night locked in each other's arms. They gave birth to a number of children who were the principal gods which controlled the forces of nature and the earth. Finally the gods rebelled against being forced to exist in a world of eternal darkness and led by Tane they forced Rangi and Papa apart and thus separated earth and sky. Tane exemplified the male element in nature and after a long search found the female element. The two elements mated and brought forth as an off-spring the Goddess of Death. Finally Tu, the God of war, united with mankind and brought forth the first mortal man, Tiki. See also gods; legends.

NECKLACES

Both men and women wore necklaces, these being of many types, each with its own name. The objects which could be strung together into necklaces included shells, human, dog and shark's teeth, stones and seeds.

Maoris also hung pendants around their neck. The most valued of these was the greenstone *tiki*. Whalebone *tiki* were also worn. Another prized form of pendant was the large tooth of the sperm whale, cut on an angle so that it resembled a tongue and furnished with two carved or inlaid eyes. Also worn was a type of sachet woven or made of skin and stuffed with sweet smelling grasses, leaves or gum, (see jade; tiki).

NOSE FLUTES (*see flute*)

ORATORY
(*whai-korero*)

As a people with a spoken instead of a written tradition, the Maoris prized greatly the art of oratory. It was an art not confined to the noble or high born, as in many cultures, but one which was encouraged in all free men. In some tribes women were even permitted to speak in the policy making councils, in other tribes women could not be heard.

The Maori had all the qualities which go to make a great orator — a love of poetry and song, a love of clowning and a sure and in-built sense of drama. Speech making and story telling were of course indulged in on many occasions but at those times when formal oratory was called for on the *marae*, the orators always carried a club as they strode to and fro making a speech and they punctuated their remarks with appropriate gestures. Normally the end of a speech was marked by a *kinaki* or relish in the form of a chanted song.

In this modern day speech making is still considered an art and follows, at least in part, many of the old forms. Mercifully however speeches are usually much shorter and will sometimes be bi-lingual with a truncated English version following the Maori.

PA

In modern usage *pa* is used to denote a collection of houses on ancestral land occupied by Maoris. There are of course now no 'villages' in the traditional sense of the term and Maoris live in the same manner as all New Zealanders. In former times a Maori village was termed *kainga* (which is also the Maori word for 'home') but once the village was protected by defensive works it was called a *pa* or fortified village. *Pa* were surrounded by palisades and earthworks and frequently terraced around, or on top of, a hill. The Maoris appeared to have a genius as military engineers and early visitors marvelled at the cunning and extent of the fortifications around the many *pa* which they found throughout the country. See marae; meeting house; whare; warfare.

PAINTING

Rock paintings are to be found more commonly in the South Island, especially in the limestone caves of North Otago and South Canterbury. In the North Island the rock designs were often engraved. The ancient Maori also used paint on himself, particularly on the face, and early visitors speak of grotesque personal adornment resulting from the use of multi-hued paint.

Maori legend tells how the art of painting the face and of painting designs on the exterior of houses was the forerunner of the arts of tattooing and wood carving respectively but there is no doubt that the Maori continued with the face painting long after the art of tattoo had been perfected. With the advent of carving however house painting seems to have been almost entirely confined to the artistic decoration of the rafters ridge poles and battens of meeting houses in the red, black and white geometrical designs shown in the accompanying illustration. The most common motif was the curvilinear fern frond design, see carving; tattoo.

PAKEHA

This is the word which the Maori used to denote the strangers who came to his land from across the seas in the late eighteenth and early nineteenth century. It is now applied by both races to denote New Zealanders who are of predominantly European blood. There is some doubt about the origin of the word but the most popular theory is that it derives from *pakehakeha*, a man-like, imaginary being with a fair skin found in Maori mythology, see *Maori*.

PATU

The patu is any type of short club. (See also mere, meremere, kotiate). All types had in common a wide striking end with sharpened edges and a rounded portion for holding in the hand. This end was pierced and threaded with a thong which went around the wrist. The clubs were used for quick in-fighting and were designed for short arm jabs to the temple, neck and ribs instead of the downward blow used with other forms of club. Thus it was normally only as the enemy fell or staggered that the handle was used to deliver a downward blow to the skull as a coup de grace.

PAUA (see shellfish)

PIPI (see shellfish)

PIUPIU

The modern dance kilt or piupiu is the only item of traditional Maori costume which is still worn and which is made roughly to the same technique as in olden times. The term *piupiu* does not seem to have been used formerly and the term *rapaki* was normally used for the kilt-like lower garment. The making of *piupiu* is time consuming and complex and it is not surprising that they command high prices nowadays. A good sized *piupiu* has some 250 lengths of flax each one of which is treated by hand.

The first step is to gather the flax. Experts use only selected blades from the heart of the flax bush. The leaves are then cut to the required length and fleshy lower portion near the base of the leaf cut away. Normally a cutting board is used and on this is marked the pattern of the garment, that is those portions which on the finished article will appear as black. The leaf is laid across the board. A sharp shell can be used for cutting and stripping the leaf but a knife will do, although it must be carefully wielded if the leaf is not to be damaged. The leaf is lightly cut across above and below those parts which are to appear in black and the shiny green surface portion of the leaf is lifted so that the white fibre is exposed.

Sometimes the garment is now put together with the leaves being fastened to a plaited top or alternatively this may be done after the dyeing stage is complete. The latter is more normal from my own experience. It is possible to dye the garment using ink but most Maori craftsmen scorn this. Most experts know of a stagnant pool with mud containing plenty of what we now know to be iron oxide. The Maori called the dye *parapara*. The flax is immersed for about a day in the pool and then sometimes for another two days in a solution formed from the pounded bark of the *hinau* and water. This fixes the dye. Finally the flax is washed out and left in the sun to dry. The normal part of the leaf curls into a straw-like cylinder and over a period of time changes to a fawn colour. The stripped parts of the leaf of course have already turned black.

POHUTUKAWA

When the Maori pronounce the word quickly the early settlers thought it sounded like "footy-cover" and at first used this word for what became known later as the NZ Christmas tree. *Pohutukawa* is a tough evergreen tree growing on steep hillsides and cliff faces down to the sea. Its brilliant red flowers bloom at Xmas time, hence the name. The Maori sometimes plucked these flowers and used them for personal adornment. A drive around the sea coast of the Eastern part of the North Island, when the tree is flowering, is of breath-taking beauty as the road snakes around mile after mile of crimson cliff faces.

POI

Few dances of the Maori people are more popular with audiences than the graceful *poi* dance. The *poi* is distinctive to the Maori of New Zealand in contrast to other dance forms such as the action song which have their counterparts elsewhere in Polynesia.

In olden times the *poi* balls were made from flax, the dressed fibre of which was woven into a fine cloth. This was wrapped around an inner core, usually of pappus from the *raupo* or bull rush. Designs were often woven in colour into the outer covering. Feathers of dog's fur were sometimes attached to the collar of the ball. When dog's hair was used the article was known as·*poi awe*.

Modern *poi* are sometimes made from traditional material but normally rather more prosaic ingredients are used. Toilet or newspaper makes a good inner filling. This filling is rolled into a ball about 3-4 inches in diameter. Beginners often prefer a somewhat larger ball than that used in concert performances. The filling is covered with unbleached calico or muslin. Shiny plastic is often preferred for stage use as it reflects the light. The material should be firmly tied or stitched and then attached to the string which should be fishing cord or twine of similar thickness with a large knot or twist of paper at the holding end. There are two types of *poi*, long *poi* for which the ball is slightly larger and which has a string about the length of the user's arm, and the short *poi* which has a smaller ball and a string of about nine inches in length.

Making A Poi

(1) Stage 1. Take a rolled up ball of paper or fabric and thread string through it, anchoring with knot at far side.
(2) Stage 2. The covering is done.
(3) Stage 3. Tie covering around the ball. Fasten firmly at collar.
(4) Stage 4. Make twist of paper at end of string for a secure hold.

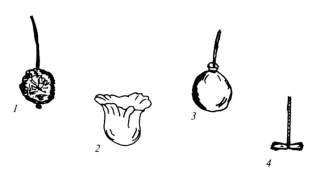

POI DANCE

(*Haka poi*)

It will be seen from the preceding heading that there were two types of *poi*, long and short. Legend recounts how the dance with the long *poi* was taught only to women of noble birth. In the end the young ladies of the less exalted classes devised the dance with the short *poi*. In olden times the dance was accompanied by a rhythmic chant. Such chants are still used but a European type tune is more usual. The dancers stand in rows but for some *poi* such as the famous *waka* or canoe *poi*, the performers sit or kneel.

Each dance consists of a number of different figures, each of which is performed for one verse of the song. We illustrate the basic figure from both the long and short *poi*. In my book "Games and Dances of the Maori People" words, music and actions are given.

The *poi* cord is held between thumb and first finger with the end of the string in the palm and the ball hanging free. The patting of the *poi* in single *poi* movements is done with the fingers or back of the hand. The tap should only be sufficient to arrest the swing of the ball and reverse its movement. The rhythm is tapped out by putting the body weight on the left foot and lightly tapping the right foot in time to the music. The long *poi* is the more simple of the two dances and the double *poi* (i.e. with a *poi* in each hand) is the easiest long *poi* movement to master.

Movement 1   Movement 2

Long Poi — The Crossed Arm Swing
(1) Swing the *poi* forward once vertically, as shown above, figure A.
(2) Cross the arms as above with the left forearm outside the right and swing the *poi* forward once again, figure B.
(3) Repeat the first movement, figure A.

Movement 3   Movement 4

Short Poi — Porotiti (Twirl)
(1) The right hand twirls the *poi* to the right whilst the left arm moves slightly from the waist so that the *poi* beats gently against the hand on downward swing, figure C.
(2) The dancer then lifts her right hand above the waist so that the *poi* hits against the back of the left hand, figure D.
(3) The two movements alternate so that the *poi* first hits the fingers of the left hand, then the back of the hand, then the fingers, then the back etc, each time marking a beat of the tune.

PUKEKO
The long legged, brightly coloured *pukeko* is the New Zealand swamp hen and is found in large numbers in the wet and swampy areas of New Zealand. The ancient Maori valued *pukeko* as food and for the feathers.

QUEEN
The so-called "Maori Queen" (Dame Te Ata-i-rangikahu) is in no sense a sovereign of all the Maori tribes, as some people suppose, but is paramount chieftainess of the Waikato tribes of the central North Island. The Maori 'King Movement' came into being in the late nineteenth century, as a focus of Maori nationalism and aspirations for the future, at a time when many thinking Maoris rightly feared for the future of their race in the face of the land hunger of the pakeha and the effect of the white man's diseases on their numbers. Dame Ata is the latest descendant of a distinguished line of leaders and as such she is honoured and respected by other tribes for her leadership of the Waikato people.

RAFTER PAINTING (*see painting*)

RANGATIRA
Maori society was broadly divided into three classes, the nobility, which of course included the chiefs or *ariki*, common people and slaves. The term *rangatira* means "well born, a chief, a person of good breeding" and as such includes both sexes. As few Maoris will admit to being not of good breeding, one cynic has said that there were only two classes — *rangatira* and slaves!

RAIN CAPE
(*Pake*)
This was the roughest and most utilitarian of Maori cloaks. It was made from *kiekie* or flax and onto the basic woven garment was attached an outer thatch of overlapping free hanging leaves which shed the water. Rain itself was regarded by the Maoris as the tears wept by Rangi the sky mother when she was forcibly separated from her embrace of Papa, the earth father, (see mythology)

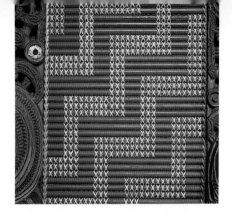

REED WORK

(tukutuku; tuitui)

Ornamental lattice work panels for the decoration of important houses was evolved by the Maori after he came to New Zealand. To meet the needs of the colder climate the sides of houses were enclosed and made as draft proof as possible. Thus close fitting side panels were evolved made from vertical rods faced with horizontal battens which were visible inside the building. These battens were painted red or black. In former times, fern stalks were used but nowadays, half rounded beading has proved an effective and more durable substitute.

The vertical and horizontal battens were lashed together with coloured fibre. These lashings consisted of dyed or bleached flax or *kiekie*, which gave black and white colours, and the yellow-orange *pingao*. The painted red battens added a fourth colour. By varying the pattern of the lashings a lattice work design was achieved. Unlike carving, the designs had to be rectilinear in composition because of the limitations of the medium. The designs were named according to the objects which they suggested to the imaginative eye. Thus triangles were called *niho taniwha* or monster's teeth whilst spaced vertical lines were *roimata* (tears) or *turuturu* (rain drops). A diamond shape was *patiki* (flounder), a zigzag *kaokao* (ribs).

Tututuku was considered women's work. It was a somewhat tedious task as thousands of lashings had to be threaded through the panels with the utmost care to as not to make any errors in the panels which would be only too apparent later to the critical eyes of the craftsmen and of the tribe. There was a complication in making the panels in ancient times. Whilst they were being constructed, meeting houses were *tapu* and no women could enter them. Thus girls could only be employed on the outside of the house to pass the strips back and forth through the battens to a man working inside. Nowadays the problem is solved by the panel being prefabricated to the required specification in some other building and being worked upon there by the women.

We illustrate one of the typical reed lattice patterns known as *kaokao* (ribs). The vertical battens which back the panel are shown on the left for illustrative purposes although these would not be visible from the interior of the house. The design is in white and black and could be copied to make an attractive hanging panel to decorate a room. Black and white wool or twine could be used in lieu of the normal fibres. If your patience or ability does not run to making a panel, it is a worthwhile exercise to try and reproduce the design on a sheet of paper. The artistry of the ancient Maori who devised such patterns without the aid of graph paper, protractors and other modern aids can thus be appreciated as well as the difficulty of executing hundreds of feet of panelling without making visible mistakes!

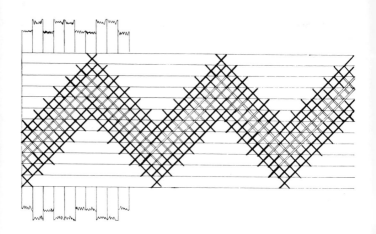

ROCK DRAWINGS (*see painting*)

RUNNING
(*omaoma*)
Running and racing against one another was not only a children's pastime but a competitive sport for adults also. It would seem however the ancient Maori preferred the marathon to the sprint. Early accounts tell of long distance races of up to fifty miles using a bent knee jog trot. The runner would go to some far off spot and leave a token or make a mark and then return to the start point. There was also a style of running in pairs with each competitor holding his partner around the neck.

SHELL FISH
Fish was a very essential source of protein food for the Maori and shell fish were as important as fish from fresh and salt water in many areas. Popular delicacies were *tio* (oyster), *kuku* (mussel), *pipi* (cockle), *kina* (sea egg), *paua* and *toheroa*. Normally it was a woman's job to collect shellfish. When plentiful the fish were eaten fresh. Otherwise they were dried for future use. They were cooked in a steam oven or placed in a heap and encircled with a ring of fire.

SLED
(reti; horua)
Sled riding was a popular sport with children and adolescents. A slide would be made on a suitable slope and water thrown on it to make it slippery. Sleds consisted either of makeshift items such as a length of bark, the head of a *ti* tree or a piece of wood, or a specially manufactured item in the form of a smooth hewn plank with a curved-up forward end which on occasions was even decorated with carving. These specially made sleds would often hold two or three children. Sometimes the under sides would be rubbed with shark oil to make them even more slippery. Childish jingles and songs were recited before the slide began. Children would compete against one another to see how far the sled would go when it reached level ground. Sometimes the slide ended in the water and thus became a water shute.

SPINNING TOP
(potaka)

Maoris played with two types of top; humming tops and whip tops. Both types were commonly made of wood but there are examples of whip tops made from stone. Humming tops were somewhat similar to today's children's tops but had an upper shaft rising from the body. The cord was wound down this shaft from the top. A flat piece of wood was used to steady the top until it was spun. Whilst spinning it emitted a humming sound. A top with a much louder hum could be made from a gourd pierced by a stick. One end of the stick formed the spinning point and the other the shaft for the string. Holes around the side of the gourd produced the noise. Whip tops were similar in shape to humming tops but had a flat top and were sometimes carved around the upper rim or on top, or decorated with *paua*. The whip was of strips of flax tied to a handle. The flax was wound tightly around the upper part of the top body and then the handle pulled so that the top fell to the ground spinning. Spinning could be prolonged by lashing the top with the whip.

Note to Illustrations

A—Whip top. Note groove on right hand side for the flax

B—Whip for top consisting of flax fibres attached to stick

C—Humming top. Note two strings wound in opposite directions around shaft so that top is spun by two people (After Edge Partington MS)

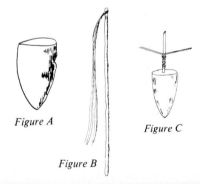

Figure A

Figure B

Figure C

STICK GAMES
(*ti rakau*)

This is another strongly rhythmical game. Today it is played in very simple form by girls. In former times it was a serious war game. There are of course many versions. In one type all but one of the players stood in a circle the remaining player went to the centre. Each person had a light rod about three foot long which they would throw at the centre player who had to catch them and throw them back at their particular owner. If the owner missed the catch, he went to the centre. An umpire ensured fair throwing. In another version the players stood in two ranks approximately ten feet apart, facing one another. One stick only was thrown back and forth and a player who missed the catch had to retire. The winner was the last remaining player.

Many forms are set to music and played with shorter sticks than those used for the war game, being thrown back and forth in various patterns in time to the music. Players may be in twos, three, fours or in a long row. These are the versions which have survived to the present day. In these the sticks have a diameter of about one inch or more and are 12 to 18 inches long. There is no element of competition and the item is more like a dance than a game. There are a number of sets or movements, each one of which is done for the length of one verse of the song. In my book "Games and Dances of the Maori People" I have given full details. There is only space to illustrate one set consisting of three movements, each of which takes one beat of a waltz tune called "E Papa". Thus the complete movement occupies one bar and is repeated for the whole 16 bar verse of the song. For each verse a different set is used.

(1) *Movement 1*. Sticks are tapped on ground
(2) *Movement 2*. Each player knocks his own sticks together
(3) *Movement 3*. Each player throws his right stick and with the same hand catches his partner's stick
(4) Movements 1 and 2 are then repeated, followed by movement 3 except that this time it is the left stick which is thrown instead of the right.

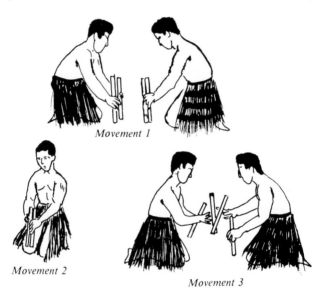

Movement 1

Movement 2

Movement 3

STRING GAMES
(*whai*)

This is a Maori version of a game which is popular with children the world over. In English it is called "cat's cradle". It is less common nowadays but formerly it was a popular game with young and old of both sexes. Women were usually more proficient than men and probably played it more often. As with all Maori games, it has its utilitarian aspect and skill with *whai* encouraged an agility with the fingers which was most necessary for the traditional female arts of weaving and tukutuku work.

In *whai* the figures are all given names and usually represent some object such as a fishing net or an incident in mythology. It had its competitive aspect in days of old. Two players would sit back to back and on a signal make a given figure. The first one finished was the winner. Medium gauge fishing cord or heavy twine should be used. Take a piece about six foot long and join it smoothly to form a loop. Now try the simple movement:

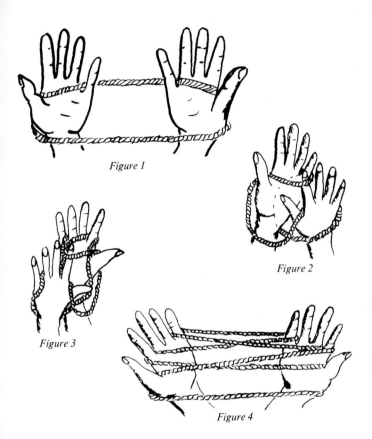

Figure 1

Figure 2

Figure 3

Figure 4

(1) Start with the string held as shown.

(2) Hook the right finger under the string which runs across the palm of the left hand and pull the string taut by parting the hands.

(3) There are now two strings running across the palm of the right hand, one from the thumb and one from around the first finger. Insert the left forefinger under the string which runs across the right palm from the thumb. Be careful not to hook up also the other string from the right forefinger.

(4) Pull the strings taut by parting the hands and you will now have figure as shown. This figure represents a rope ladder. It is also the basic figure from which other more complicated figures are made.

TAIAHA

The *taiaha* is often mistaken for a spear but it was never intended to be thrown. It was in reality a long club, similar to the English quarter staff, and was one of the principal weapons of the Maori warrior. *Taiaha* were made from light, strong, dense-grained wood and ideally weighed no more than 1-2 lbs. The pointed end known as *arero* or tongue was often carved and decorated. From the tongue the shaft ran for some 5-6 feet, lessening in thickness and widening out to about 3-4 inches. The *taiaha* was carried and wielded with the blade uppermost. It could thus be used to parry an enemy weapon and to strike at the head or body. As the opponent fell the *arero* could be used to slash and pierce the unguarded stomach. Experienced warriors always watched their opponent's muscles rather than his weapon and could tell when a blow was about to be delivered by the flexing of the muscles. See mere, patu; warfare.

TAKAHE

The rare and beautiful takahe was thought for many years to be extinct until in 1948 a colony was located in a remote part of Fiordland National Park in the south of the South Island. This area has now been set aside as a sanctuary for the takahe and a few also are held in captivity. Like the *kiwi* the *takahe* is flightless but it is a swift runner. It is not unlike the *pukeko*. The Maoris used the bird for food and prized its coloured feathers, (see *pukeko*)

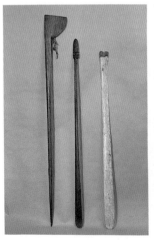 

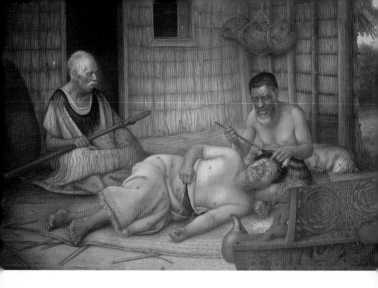

TAPU

The law of *tapu* was a whole series of prohibitions which governed the daily and religious life of the ancient Maori. It related to things, persons and places and items which were *tapu* were sacred and to some degree forbidden. For example in some respects a house was *tapu* and therefore cooked food was never eaten inside nor rainwater collected from its roof. A burial ground was *tapu* for ordinary purposes. Warriors about to go into battle and thus dedicated to the war god were *tapu* and could not sleep with their wives. Anyone who violated *tapu* placed himself in the greatest danger and elaborate rites known as *whakanoa* (literally 'to make free'), were necessary to lift the *tapu* from any person or object.

TATTOOING
(*ta moko*)

The designs used in Maori tattooing were similar to those in wood carving and curvilinear motifs predominated. Tattoo was regarded purely as adornment. It did not denote rank nor was it considered proof of fortitude. Nevertheless it was so painful that it was only carried out on adults and usually over a long period of time. Men were more heavily tattooed than women and many had designs covering their faces, body, .buttocks and thighs. On women it was usually confined to the chins and lips, although sometimes women had tattooed bands on their ankles and wrists, their foreheads and, even more rarely, the breasts. The tattooist used a bone chisel or comb which he tapped with a mallet. After the skin was pierced, the blood was wiped away and a bluish pigment rubbed into the incision.

TIKI

Tiki was the first man (see mythology) and wood carvings of men are called *tiki*. *Heitiki* (*hei* 'hanging', *tiki* 'the human form') was a neck pendant of a particular design. It was a curiously cramped image of the human form, usually female, with the limbs drawn up and fitting around and over the body and not protruding from it. The head was also turned to one side to preserve the generally rounded oblong shape of the design and the eyes and tongue were prominent. *Tiki* were carved from wood (possible a more modern development), stone, bone and those which were especially prized, from greenstone. *Heitiki* were considered as the momento of an ancestor or series of ancestors and as they were passed from generation to generation they gained value through contact with those who had gone before, (see also necklaces).

TOHEROA   (see shellfish)

TOHUNGA

Tohunga were experts in any area of knowledge. Hence the tattooist was a *tohunga ta moko*, (see tattooing), and an expert wood carver was a *tohunga whakairo*. However the term is usually thought of nowadays as applying to a priest or expert in the religious arts of the Maori. There are still a few men with reputations as tohunga to be found amongst the modern day Maori. However the modern tohunga is more in the nature of a faith healer.

In former times tohunga were graded according to the class of gods they served (see gods). Those of the highest class underwent a long and difficult course in a proper school of instruction and were credited with an ability to control the elements with sorcery, benign or otherwise. Those who were thought to practise black magic however were feared and detested. The high class tohunga were also the repository of tribal law, myths and history and were expert geneologists. One authority has called them the scholars, scientists and philosophers, as well as the theologians, of ancient Maoridom.

TRIBE
(*iwi*)

The smallest Maori social unit was the family (which see). Groups of closely related family were *hapu* or sub-tribes and all those sub-tribes descended from a common ancestor were members of an *iwi* or tribe. In the course of time some of the sub-tribes themselves became so enlarged that they split up into sub-tribes. The tie between the *hapu* of a tribe was strong and despite occasional quarrels hapu would combine in tribal matters under the chief of the whole tribe. Tribes from a common ancestor formed a looser confederation amongst whom there was an occasional community of interest. Although they might periodically fight bitterly with one another they would almost always band together against the common enemy. Extending beyond this was the tie between tribes who although they did not share a common ancestor, the families of their particular ancestors had come to New Zealand in the same canoe. Thus, for example, there is the bond between the tribes of the Arawa confederation such as Ngati Whakaue and Ngati Pikiao because they shared the same ancestor, and between the Arawa tribes and Ngati Tuwharetoa because that respective ancestors had voyaged together.

TRUMPET
(*pu*)

There are four types of trumpet, those made from flax, those made from wood, those made from shell and those made from gourd. Flax trumpets were really only a child's toy being a flax leaf wound to resemble a megaphone. Shell trumpets were more sophisticated and often had a wooden mouthpiece. They did not produce music but were used as a means of summoning attention to assemble the community, to announce visitors and, in some tribes, to herald the birth of a first-born son. Wooden trumpets ranged from two to eight feet long and had a bell shape at one end which might be made separately and attached. The wood trumpet was usually a war trumpet used by troops during battle or to warn against attack. There is dispute as to whether the trumpet made from a gourd was used in New Zealand but, although there is no material evidence in the form of extant articles, it seems likely that the Maori would see the possibilities of the gourd for this purpose and use it in this way as in the rest of Polynesia.

TUATARA
The tuatara is said to be the last survivor of the huge reptiles of the Stone Age such as the dinosaur and the brontosaurus. It is native to New Zealand and has the chameleon properties of many lizards.

TUI
When the pakeha came to New Zealand he called the tui "parson bird" because of the distinctive ruffle of white feathers at its throat. The bird is a wonderful singer but it can also mimic other birds and the male bird can be taught to speak. The Maoris prized the tui not only for its flesh and its feathers but also as a pet. It would be kept secluded from other sounds and the same words repeated until the tui could produce them. There are accounts of Maoris carrying them on their shoulders from which perch the tui would greet visitors with the words they had learned.

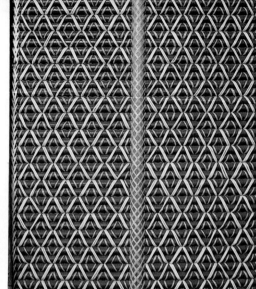

TUKUTUKU

Tukutuku refers to the lattice work decorative wall panels to be found in the houses, both individual and community, of the Maori. The shiny stalks of the *kakaho* flower were placed horizontally and woven with reeds to form distinctive patterns. See also reed work.

UMU

The Maori cooking pit or earth oven was termed *umu*. It was usually sheltered fom the elements by the *whare umu* with its open end walls to allow smoke to escape. Here was stored the impedimenta of cooking and the *whare umu* would also be used for sleeping by the slaves and menials. In addition however to its purely functional use, the *umu* also had a place in ceremonial and religious functions and thus the word for oven became associated with the rite itself as in *umu tamoe* which was a ritual to deprive enemies of power. In ritual ovens, the oven and the food itself were purely symbolic so an oven of only about six inches in diameter might be used to cook a single sweet potato. In contrast was the oven used for "fire" walking which was much larger than the normal cooking oven so that the hot stones could be spread evenly over a large surface. (The celebrants walked on hot stones in actuality, not on fire).

VILLAGE (*see pa*)

VIRGIN
(*puhi*)

Sexual experimentation from adolescence until marriage was regarded as normal and desirable by the ancient Maori, hence virgins of either sex were virtually non-existant after the early teens at the latest. However there were occasionally to be found *puhi* maidens. These were high born young ladies who had been betrothed by their parents at an early age to a specific suitor or whom the parents had decided to keep virginal until such time as a suitable match could be made. To guard them from the temptations of the flesh as well as the unsought ravages of passionate young men, *puhi* were constantly attended by other young women of high rank. Nevertheless accidents did happen and there are sad stories of the fall from grace of *puhi*. Some *puhi* were established as objects designed to enhance tribal prestige. The fame of such young women would be spread abroad and prospective suitors would come from afar to display their looks and athletic prowess as well as their wealth. The coming of suitors would be regarded as an occasion for feasting and social intercourse. One authority describes the function of such *puhi* as "a sort of carnival queen who by her beauty and graces enhanced the prestige of her people." Once a suitable young man had been selected; the consent of the girl's parents and brothers was necessary but in the case of a tribal *puhi* the tribal authorities would possibly also have a say in the matter.

WARFARE
(*pakanga*)

Few races were more warlike than the Maori of old and the histories of the tribes are full of stories of military campaigns for reasons of prestige, tribal gain and even for recreation. The Maori was both a mobile fighter, adept at ambushing, patrolling and raiding, and an exponent of positional warfare involving attacks on a large scale or alternatively lengthy defensive battles and sieges. He was also a skilful engineer (see *pa*). Despite his ferocity, the Maori was also a courageous and chivalrous opponent. History contains many examples of consideration for the wounded, safe conduct of women and children from sieges and occasionally temporary halts in the battle so that beleaguered garrisons could obtain fresh supplies in order to continue the battle!

WARRIOR
(*toa*)

In ancient Maoridom every citizen was a soldier and tribes were safe from marauders only if military prowess made them so. Although women could, and did, fight to defend their homes, warfare was considered a man's game. From earliest childhood young men were trained in the military arts and even their games had as a secondary object the inculcation of military skills and prowess.

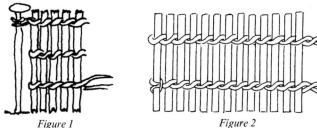

| Figure 1 | Figure 2 |

Single pair twining attached to weaving stick

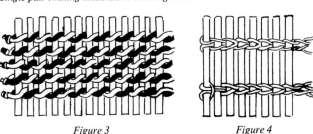

| Figure 3 | Figure 4 |

WEAVING
(*whatu*)

Maori weaving would probably be regarded by some as plaiting since the threads are manipulated by the fingers and neither a loom or shuttle is used as with conventional weaving as pakeha know it. The flax leaf was pounded until the fibre could be separated and then this was rolled into a fine twine between the palm and thigh of the weaver. To form the "loom", two sticks called *turuturu* were driven into the ground a sufficient distance apart to take the width of the item which was to be woven. (see figure 1.)

Spaced single pair twining (figure 2) was used for rough garments such as rain capes. The technique was very simple with the twine being woven at regular intervals around the flax leaves as shown in the diagram. The vertical threads were warps and the horizontal ones were the weft. The interspacing varied according to the type of garment but was regular throughout the garment. When the weaving approached ground level the lowest weft row was raised up to the upper end of the sticks.

A development from the spaced technique was close single pair twining (figure 3). In this technique the weft rows were woven as close together as possible to produce a heavy strong material similar to canvas. This technique was used for undecorated war cloaks, for dogskin cloaks in which long narrow strips of dogskin with the hair facing out were sewn in vertical strips to completely cover the base material and for tufted dog's hair cloaks in which the material was covered with teased out tufts of the long hair from the tail.

A further development was the two pair weft (figure 4) which arose from the need for better garments. With the two pair weft a long pair of threads was doubled around the first warp to form a back and a front weft. The back pair was opened and the front pair passed between its two threads, then both pairs were drawn tight. The two wefts had now crossed so that the back weft was in front. Over the next warp the process was reversed and so on.

A thick three ply braid was used to finish the neck border in all capes. When the weft row reached the desired width of the garment, it was tied around the last warp with a reef knot. A refinement was the insertion of short weft rows during the weaving at appropriate places to form slight bulges in those parts of a cloak which fitted over the buttocks and shoulders. By this technique the cloak hung properly and did not gape in front.

Learning the art of weaving was attended with appropriate ceremony and *tapu*. Usually the pupil was female but sometimes men would be taught. Strangely, the teacher was always a tohunga and male.

WHARE
Most family houses or *whare* were small with a tiny door through which the occupants crawled. As they were only considered sleeping places they were rarely high enough to allow a person to stand upright. They had wooden frames and the walls and roof were of tightly woven dry grass and flax to exclude as far as possible the drafts of winter. The fireplace was in the middle of the floor enclosed by stones and the people slept around it on grass or fern and covered themselves with woven cloaks or mats. Each village had a meeting house (which see) for community gatherings and to accommodate visitors. Most *whare* had verandahs and it was here that the occupants would sit during the daylight hours.

XMAS
Kirihimete was of course introduced by the missionaries when they brought the Christian religion to New Zealand. The Maoris avidly embraced Christianity and within a short time of the colonisation of the country the Maori population was almost entirely Christian.

YEAR
(*tau*)

The Maoris recognised the cycle of the seasons which represented the passing of a year although they lacked a precise unit of measuring time. *Tau* probably meant "season" in pre-European times. They were able to fix time by the sun and at night by the stars. Up to one year they managed well. After that the only unit was the imprecise one of a human generation.

YOUTH
(*taitamariki*)

As in all communities, youth was a time for learning by young Maoris. There was certain knowledge of course instilled from earliest childhood — respect for elders and betters, knowledge of *tapu* and of the practices appropriate to various social occasions, tribal history, custom and folklore. During adolescence boys and girls learned occupational skills by helping their parents. Boys were initiated into such masculine activities as hunting, fishing, agriculture, building and the like, whilst girls learned cooking, plaiting, weaving etc. Boys also were taught the arts of war. Higher education for selected youths, usually the sons of chiefs and priests, was given in the *whare wananga* or houses of learning. Here the more esoteric aspects of tribal law and ritual were taught. Other youths were taught to become master craftsmen in such skilled crafts as carving, tattooing and agriculture.

ZITHER
(*ku*)

We have had to allow ourselves some slight poetic latitude in search for an association with Maoridom beginning with the letter 'z'! However, a stringed instrument which can be distantly associated with the zither was reported by Canon Stack, an early visitor to New Zealand. According to Stack it was called *ku* and made from hardwood. It was about ten inches long and the single string of flax fibre produced sound when it was tapped.

NEW ZEALAND POCKET GUIDES

CAKE DECORATING GUIDE — Book One (S049) .... Dorothy Beatty
FLORA AND FAUNA OF NEW ZEALAND (S032) .... Glen Pownall
JADE TREASURES OF THE MAORI (S090) .... Murdoch Riley
KIWI AND MOA — Two unique Birds (S071) .... Murdoch Riley
KIWI COOKBOOK — N.Z. Recipes (S016) .... Alan Armstrong
KNOW YOUR MAORI CARVING (S069) .... Glen Pownall
KNOW YOUR NEW ZEALAND BIRDS (S068) .... Murdoch Riley
MAORI CUSTOMS AND CRAFTS (S009) .... Alan Armstrong
MAORI LEGENDS — Retold (S017) .... Alistair Campbell
MAORI SONGBOOK — Traditional Songs (S014) .... Sam Freedman
N.Z. TREES AND FERNS (S073) .... Murdoch Riley
N.Z. WAY WITH FLOWERS (S075) .... Eileen Dobson
N.Z. WILDLIFE — Sea and Land (S070) .... Murdoch Riley
SAY IT IN MAORI — Phrasebook (S010) .... Alan Armstrong
SHRUBS AND SMALL TREES (S076) .... Murdoch Riley
SUCCESSFUL CAKE DECORATING — Book Two (S074) .... Dorothy Beatty
WEKA WON'T LEARN — For children (S047) .... Maxine Schur

NEW ZEALAND BOOKS

GAMES AND DANCES OF THE MAORI PEOPLE — (B088).... Alan Armstrong
HINEMOA AND TUTANEKAI (B045)................................. Harold Callender
JADE TREASURES OF THE MAORI — Large Format (B089).... Murdoch Riley
MAORI GAMES — English language (B039)................................. Colin Deed
MAORI GAMES — Maori language (B040) .... Colin Deed
MAORI PEOPLE — Essay and pictures (B037) .... Jim Siers
MOANA — Early New Zealand (B030)............................... Barry Mitcalfe
MUSIC OF THE MAORI (B034)... Dr Barrow
NEATH THE MANTLE OF RANGI (B036).................................. Brian Enting
N.Z. SHELLS AND SHELLFISH (B054).................................. Glen Pownall
N.Z. TREES AND FERNS — Hardback (B072) .... Murdoch Riley
PRIMITIVE ART OF THE N.Z. MAORI (B013)............................ Glen Pownall
SURFRIDING IN NEW ZEALAND — 3rd Edition (B091).......... Wayne Warwick
UNIQUE NEW ZEALAND (B003) .... Glen Pownall
WITCH AT THE WELLINGTON LIBRARY (B066) .... Maxine Schur

CASSETTE/POCKET GUIDE COMBINATIONS

HAERE MAI! — 20 musical tracks + 30 page 'How to perform action songs, haka, poi, etc.' + booklet (VPS475C)

BIRDS OF NEW ZEALAND — 18 bird calls + 64 page 'Know your New Zealand Birds' (VPS445CB)

HERITAGE OF MAORI SONG — Words and music to 28 songs in booklet + actual songs on cassette (SPR40C)